Mastering Money: A Fun Guide to Personal Finance

Financial Planning, Volume 2

Karen Snow

Published by Karen Snow, 2024.

While every precaution has been taken in the preparation of this book, the publisher assumes no responsibility for errors or omissions, or for damages resulting from the use of the information contained herein.

MASTERING MONEY: A FUN GUIDE TO PERSONAL FINANCE

First edition. July 15, 2024.

Copyright © 2024 Karen Snow.

Written by Karen Snow.

Table of Contents

Introduction 1

Chapter 1: Understanding Money 3

Chapter 2: Budgeting Basics 6

Chapter 3: Smart Saving Strategies 9

Chapter 4: Managing Debt Wisely 12

Chapter 5: Investing for Beginners 16

Chapter 6: Planning for Retirement 20

Chapter 7: Protecting Your Finances 24

Chapter 8: Taxes Made Simple 28

Chapter 9: Building Wealth 32

Chapter 10: Financial Planning for Families 36

Chapter 11: Navigating Major Life Events 40

Chapter 12: Financial Freedom and Independence 44

Chapter 13: Continuing Your Financial Journey 48

Introduction

Money is a big part of our lives. We use it every day to buy things we need and want. But do you know how to make the most out of your money? This book is here to help you learn all about personal finance in a fun and easy way. We'll cover everything from understanding money to budgeting, saving, and even investing. By the end of this book, you'll have the skills to manage your money wisely and achieve your financial goals.

Personal finance might sound complicated, but it's really just about making smart decisions with your money. Whether you're saving for a new toy, planning for college, or dreaming of buying a house someday, understanding how to manage your money is essential. This book will break down these concepts into simple, easy-to-understand steps, so you can start making smart financial choices today.

Have you ever wondered why some people seem to have more money than others? It's not just about how much you earn; it's also about how you manage what you have. In this book, we'll explore different ways to save and invest money, so you can grow your wealth over time. We'll also look at common financial mistakes and how to avoid them.

Money isn't just about buying things; it's also about security and freedom. When you know how to handle your finances, you can avoid debt, build savings, and plan for the future. This book will show you how to create a budget, save for emergencies, and invest wisely. With these tools, you'll be able to take control of your financial future.

Setting financial goals is a key part of managing your money. Whether you're aiming to save for a big purchase, pay off debt, or invest for the future, having clear goals can help you stay focused and motivated. This book will guide you through the process of setting and achieving your financial goals, step by step.

Throughout this book, you'll find practical tips and real-life examples to help you understand the concepts better. We'll also share stories of people who have successfully managed their finances and achieved their goals. By learning from their experiences, you can avoid common pitfalls and make smarter financial decisions.

One of the most important lessons you'll learn in this book is the power of saving. Saving money regularly, even in small amounts, can add up over time and give you financial security. We'll explore different saving strategies and show you how to make saving a habit.

Investing is another key topic we'll cover. Investing your money can help it grow faster than just saving it in a bank. We'll explain the basics of investing, including stocks, bonds, and mutual funds, and how to choose the right investments for your goals.

Budgeting is a fundamental skill for managing your money. A budget helps you keep track of your income and expenses, so you know exactly where your money is going. We'll show you how to create a budget that works for you and your lifestyle, and how to stick to it.

Understanding credit is also crucial. Credit can be a useful tool if used wisely, but it can also lead to debt if you're not careful. We'll explain how credit works, how to build good credit, and how to avoid common credit pitfalls.

Throughout this book, we'll emphasize the importance of financial literacy. Knowing how to manage your money can give you confidence and freedom. It's a skill that will benefit you for the rest of your life. By the end of this book, you'll have a solid understanding of personal finance and be well on your way to achieving your financial goals.

Chapter 1: Understanding Money

Money is something we all use every day, but have you ever stopped to think about what it really is? Money is a tool that allows us to buy goods and services. It comes in many forms, from coins and paper bills to digital currency. But no matter what form it takes, money is an essential part of our lives.

The history of money is fascinating. Long ago, people didn't use money at all. Instead, they bartered, trading goods and services directly. For example, if you were a farmer with extra corn, you might trade it with a fisherman for some fish. But bartering had its limitations. What if the fisherman didn't want your corn? That's where money came in. People started using items like shells, beads, and metal coins as a medium of exchange, making trade much easier.

Today, we use many different forms of money. In addition to coins and paper bills, we have digital money, such as the balances in our bank accounts and electronic payments we make with our credit and debit cards. Digital money has made transactions faster and more convenient, but it's still important to understand the basics of how money works.

One of the most important concepts in personal finance is how money is earned. Most people earn money by working at a job. When you work, your employer pays you a salary or wage in exchange for your time and skills. But there are other ways to earn money too, such as starting your own business, investing, or even doing chores and tasks for others.

Money plays a big role in our everyday lives. We use it to buy food, clothing, and other necessities. We also use it to pay for services like healthcare, education, and entertainment. Understanding how to manage your money well can help you make sure you have enough for the things you need and want.

To manage your money effectively, it's important to understand some basic financial terms. For example, income is the money you earn, while expenses are the money you spend. Savings are the money you set aside for future use, and investments are the money you put into something with the expectation that it will grow over time.

Banks play a crucial role in the financial system. A bank is a place where you can deposit your money for safekeeping. Banks offer various services, including checking and savings accounts, loans, and investment products. When you deposit money in a bank, the bank can lend it out to others, helping to keep the economy moving.

Saving money is important because it provides a safety net for the future. There are different types of savings accounts, each with its own benefits. A regular savings account is a safe place to keep your money and earn a small amount of interest. A high-yield savings account offers a higher interest rate, but may have more restrictions.

Interest is a key concept in personal finance. When you save money in a bank, the bank pays you interest as a reward for keeping your money there. This interest can help your savings grow over time. There are two main types of interest: simple interest and compound interest. Simple interest is calculated only on the principal amount, while compound interest is calculated on both the principal and the interest already earned.

Credit and debit are two common ways to pay for things. A credit card allows you to borrow money from the bank to make purchases, which you then pay back later, usually with interest. A debit card, on the other hand, allows you to spend money directly from your bank account. Both have their advantages and disadvantages, and it's important to use them wisely.

Loans are another way to borrow money. When you take out a loan, you receive a lump sum of money that you agree to pay back over time, usually with interest. There are many types of loans, including personal loans, mortgages, and student loans. It's important to understand the terms of a loan and borrow responsibly.

Budgeting is a key skill for managing your money. A budget is a plan that helps you track your income and expenses, so you can make sure you're living within your means. Creating a budget involves listing all your sources of income and all your expenses, then making adjustments as needed to stay on track.

Tracking your expenses is an important part of budgeting. By keeping a record of what you spend, you can see where your money is going and identify areas where you can cut back. There are many tools available to help you track your expenses, from simple spreadsheets to budgeting apps.

Financial planning is about setting goals for your money and making a plan to achieve them. This might include saving for a big purchase, paying off debt, or investing for the future. A good financial plan can help you stay focused and motivated, and make smarter financial decisions.

Financial literacy is the knowledge and skills needed to manage your money effectively. This includes understanding how to save, invest, and budget, as well as knowing how to avoid common financial pitfalls. Improving your financial literacy can give you confidence and control over your financial future.

In summary, understanding money and how it works is the first step to managing your finances effectively. By learning the basics of money, saving, budgeting, and investing, you can take control of your financial future and achieve your goals. This book will guide you through each of these topics in more detail, so you can become a master of your money.

Chapter 2: Budgeting Basics

Budgeting is one of the most important skills you can learn when it comes to managing your money. A budget is simply a plan for how you will spend and save your money. It helps you keep track of your income and expenses, so you can make sure you're living within your means and reaching your financial goals.

Creating a budget might sound boring, but it can actually be quite empowering. When you know where your money is going, you can make better decisions about how to use it. A budget can help you avoid debt, save for the future, and make sure you have enough money for the things that matter most to you.

The first step in creating a budget is to figure out your income. This includes any money you earn from work, as well as other sources of income like gifts, allowances, or investment earnings. Once you know how much money you have coming in, you can start to plan how you will use it.

Next, you'll need to list your expenses. These are the things you spend money on, like food, housing, transportation, and entertainment. It's helpful to categorize your expenses into different groups, such as fixed expenses and variable expenses. Fixed expenses are the same every month, like rent or a car payment, while variable expenses can change, like groceries or utilities.

Once you have a list of your income and expenses, you can start to create your budget. Begin by subtracting your fixed expenses from your income. This will give you an idea of how much money you have left for variable expenses and savings. It's important to be realistic about your expenses and make sure you're not overspending in any one area.

One popular budgeting method is the 50/30/20 rule. This suggests that you should spend 50% of your income on needs, 30% on wants, and save the remaining 20%. Needs are things like housing, food, and transportation, while wants are things like dining out, entertainment, and vacations. This rule can help you balance your spending and make sure you're saving enough for the future.

Tracking your spending is an essential part of budgeting. By keeping a record of what you spend, you can see where your money is going and make adjustments as needed. There are many tools available to help you track your spending, from simple spreadsheets to budgeting apps. Find a method that works for you and stick with it.

Setting financial goals is another important part of budgeting. Whether you're saving for a big purchase, paying off debt, or building an emergency fund, having clear goals can help you stay focused and motivated. Make sure your goals are specific, measurable, and achievable, and create a plan to reach them.

Saving money is a key part of any budget. An emergency fund is a savings account that you can use for unexpected expenses, like a car repair or medical bill. It's important to have an emergency fund to protect yourself from financial setbacks. Aim to save enough to cover three to six months of living expenses.

Living within your means is a fundamental principle of budgeting. This means spending less than you earn and avoiding debt. It can be tempting to buy things you can't afford, but living within your means will help you build financial security and avoid stress.

Avoiding impulse purchases is another important budgeting tip. It's easy to get caught up in the moment and buy something you don't really need. Before making a purchase, ask yourself if it's something you really need or if it's just a want. If it's a want, consider waiting a few days to see if you still want it.

Managing unexpected expenses is a crucial part of budgeting. No matter how carefully you plan, there will always be unexpected costs. Having an emergency fund can help you handle these expenses without derailing your budget.

A flexible budget is one that can adapt to changes in your income or expenses. Life is unpredictable, and your budget should be able to accommodate changes. If your income goes down, you'll need to adjust your spending. If your expenses go up, you may need to cut back in other areas.

Family budgeting can be a bit more complex, but it's just as important. When you have a family, you need to consider everyone's needs and make sure you're all on the same page. Involve your family in the budgeting process and teach your kids about money management.

Budgeting for different life stages is also important. Your financial needs and goals will change as you move through life. For example, your budget in college will be different from your budget when you start your first job, buy a house, or have kids. Adjust your budget as your life changes to make sure it still works for you.

Common budgeting mistakes include not tracking your spending, not having clear goals, and not being realistic about your expenses. Avoid these mistakes by keeping a close eye on your finances and making adjustments as needed.

Staying motivated with budgeting can be challenging, but it's important to stick with it. Celebrate your successes and remind yourself of your goals. If you find budgeting difficult, try to make it more fun by setting challenges or rewards for yourself.

In summary, budgeting is a powerful tool for managing your money. It helps you keep track of your income and expenses, set financial goals, and make sure you're living within your means. By creating and sticking to a budget, you can achieve financial security and reach your financial goals.

Chapter 3: Smart Saving Strategies

Saving money is one of the most important habits you can develop. It provides a safety net for the future and helps you achieve your financial goals. Whether you're saving for a big purchase, an emergency fund, or your future, having a smart saving strategy is essential.

One of the first steps to saving money is to make it a habit. This means setting aside a portion of your income regularly, even if it's just a small amount. The key is consistency. Over time, even small savings can add up to a significant amount.

There are many different saving strategies you can use to reach your goals. One popular method is the 50/30/20 rule, which suggests you save 20% of your income. Another strategy is to automate your savings, so a portion of your income is automatically transferred to your savings account each month.

High-yield savings accounts offer a higher interest rate than regular savings accounts, which can help your savings grow faster. These accounts may have more restrictions, but they're a good option if you want to earn more interest on your savings.

Certificates of deposit (CDs) are another way to save money. A CD is a type of savings account that requires you to leave your money in the account for a fixed period of time. In return, you earn a higher interest rate. CDs are a good option if you have money you don't need to access right away.

Saving for big purchases, like a car or a vacation, requires planning and discipline. Set a savings goal and create a plan to reach it. Break your goal down into smaller, manageable steps, and track your progress along the way.

The power of small savings should not be underestimated. Even small amounts of money can add up over time. Look for ways to cut down on unnecessary expenses, like dining out or buying coffee every day, and put that money into your savings.

Using coupons and discounts is another way to save money. Look for deals and sales when shopping, and use coupons whenever possible. This can help you save money on everyday purchases and free up more money for your savings.

DIY (do it yourself) can also save you money. Instead of paying someone to do something for you, consider doing it yourself. This could include things like home repairs, cooking, or even making gifts. Not only can this save you money, but it can also be a fun and rewarding experience.

Energy-saving tips can help you reduce your utility bills and save money. Simple changes, like turning off lights when you leave a room, using energy-efficient appliances, and adjusting your thermostat, can make a big difference in your energy costs.

Meal planning and grocery savings can also help you save money. Plan your meals for the week and make a shopping list before you go to the store. This can help you avoid impulse purchases and reduce food waste. Look for sales and buy in bulk when it makes sense.

Transportation cost savings are another area to consider. Carpooling, using public transportation, or biking instead of driving can save you money on gas and car maintenance. If you have to drive, keep your car well-maintained to improve fuel efficiency.

Entertainment on a budget doesn't have to be boring. Look for free or low-cost activities, like visiting parks, museums, or community events. You can also have fun at home with movie nights, game nights, or DIY projects.

Shopping smart means being mindful of your purchases. Before buying something, ask yourself if it's something you really need or if it's just a want. Compare prices and look for deals to make sure you're getting the best value for your money.

The importance of frugality is about being mindful of your spending and looking for ways to save money. This doesn't mean being cheap or depriving yourself, but rather making thoughtful choices about how you spend your money.

Delayed gratification is a powerful saving strategy. Instead of buying something immediately, wait a few days to see if you still want it. This can help you avoid impulse purchases and save money for things that truly matter to you.

Setting up sinking funds can help you save for specific goals. A sinking fund is a separate savings account for a particular purpose, like a vacation or a new car. This allows you to save gradually over time and avoid dipping into your main savings.

Retirement savings is a crucial part of any saving strategy. The earlier you start saving for retirement, the more time your money has to grow. Contribute to retirement accounts like a 401(k) or IRA and take advantage of employer matching if available.

Saving for education, whether for yourself or your children, is also important. Education can be expensive, but saving early can help reduce the financial burden. Look into education savings accounts, like a 529 plan, to help you save for college.

Building a savings cushion provides a financial safety net for unexpected expenses. Aim to save enough to cover three to six months of living expenses. This can help you avoid debt and stay on track with your financial goals.

Celebrating savings milestones can help you stay motivated. Set smaller goals along the way and celebrate when you reach them. This can make saving more fun and rewarding.

In summary, smart saving strategies are essential for achieving your financial goals. By making saving a habit, using different saving methods, and being mindful of your spending, you can build financial security and reach your goals.

Chapter 4: Managing Debt Wisely

Debt is a common part of personal finance, but managing it wisely is crucial to your financial health. Debt can be helpful in certain situations, like buying a house or paying for education, but it can also lead to financial trouble if not handled properly. Understanding how to manage debt is an important skill.

Debt comes in many forms, including credit card debt, student loans, car loans, and mortgages. Each type of debt has its own terms and conditions, and it's important to understand them before borrowing money. Knowing the interest rates, repayment terms, and any fees associated with the debt can help you make informed decisions.

Good debt is debt that can help you achieve your financial goals, like a mortgage or a student loan. These types of debt are often considered investments because they can increase your net worth or earning potential. However, it's important to borrow responsibly and only take on debt you can afford to repay.

Bad debt is debt that doesn't provide any long-term benefits, like credit card debt used to buy non-essential items. This type of debt can quickly become unmanageable if not paid off promptly. It's important to avoid accumulating bad debt and to pay off any existing bad debt as quickly as possible.

Credit cards can be a convenient way to pay for things, but they can also lead to debt if not used wisely. When you use a credit card, you're borrowing money from the bank and agreeing to pay it back later, usually with interest. If you don't pay off your balance in full each month, the interest charges can add up quickly.

One strategy for paying off credit card debt is the snowball method. This involves paying off your smallest debts first, then using the money you were paying on those debts to tackle larger ones. This can help you build momentum and stay motivated as you see your debts disappearing.

Another strategy is the avalanche method, which focuses on paying off debts with the highest interest rates first. This can save you more money in the long run because you'll pay less interest overall. Both methods have their advantages, so choose the one that works best for you.

Debt consolidation is another option for managing debt. This involves combining multiple debts into a single loan with a lower interest rate. This can make it easier to manage your payments and reduce the amount of interest you pay. However, it's important to read the terms carefully and make sure it's the right choice for your situation.

Refinancing loans can also help you manage debt. This involves taking out a new loan with better terms to pay off an existing loan. For example, if interest rates have dropped since you took out your mortgage, refinancing could lower your monthly payments and save you money over time.

Your credit score is an important factor in managing debt. A good credit score can help you qualify for lower interest rates and better loan terms. To improve your credit score, make sure to pay your bills on time, keep your credit card balances low, and avoid opening too many new accounts at once.

If you're struggling with debt, there are resources available to help you. Credit counseling services can provide advice and assistance with managing your debts. They can help you create a budget, negotiate with creditors, and develop a plan to pay off your debts.

It's also important to know your legal rights related to debt. There are laws in place to protect consumers from unfair debt collection practices. If you're being harassed by debt collectors, you have the right to ask them to stop contacting you and to dispute any errors on your credit report.

Payday loans are a type of short-term loan that can be very expensive. They often come with high interest rates and fees, making them a risky option for borrowing money. It's best to avoid payday loans if possible and look for other ways to cover unexpected expenses.

Student loans can be a valuable investment in your future, but it's important to borrow responsibly. Look for loans with low interest rates and flexible repayment options. If you have trouble repaying your student loans, explore options like income-driven repayment plans or loan forgiveness programs.

Mortgage debt is another common type of debt. A mortgage is a loan used to buy a house, and it usually comes with a long repayment term. Managing your mortgage payments and staying on top of your home maintenance costs is essential for keeping your financial situation stable.

Car loans are another type of debt that many people take on. When buying a car, it's important to consider the total cost, including interest, taxes, and fees. Make sure to shop around for the best loan terms and avoid borrowing more than you can afford to repay.

Personal loans can be used for a variety of purposes, but they should be used wisely. Before taking out a personal loan, consider whether it's really necessary and if there are other ways to achieve your goal without borrowing money.

Avoiding debt traps is crucial for maintaining your financial health. Debt traps are situations where it's easy to borrow money but difficult to repay it, like high-interest credit cards or payday loans. Be cautious about taking on new debt and always read the terms and conditions carefully.

Building an emergency fund can help you avoid debt. An emergency fund is a savings account that you can use for unexpected expenses, like car repairs or medical bills. Having an emergency fund can give you peace of mind and prevent you from relying on credit cards or loans in a crisis.

Financial discipline is essential for managing debt. This means making a commitment to live within your means, avoid unnecessary spending, and prioritize paying off your debts. It can be challenging, but the rewards are worth it.

If you're overwhelmed by debt, don't be afraid to seek professional help. Financial advisors, credit counselors, and debt management programs can provide guidance and support. They can help you create a plan to pay off your debts and get your finances back on track.

In summary, managing debt wisely is an important part of personal finance. By understanding the different types of debt, using strategies to pay off debt, and practicing financial discipline, you can take control of your finances and achieve your goals.

Chapter 5: Investing for Beginners

Investing is a powerful way to grow your money over time. While saving money is important, investing can help your money grow faster by earning returns through interest, dividends, and capital gains. Investing might seem complicated, but it doesn't have to be. This chapter will guide you through the basics of investing and help you get started.

The first step to investing is understanding why you should invest. Investing can help you achieve long-term financial goals, like buying a house, paying for education, or saving for retirement. By investing your money, you can take advantage of compound interest and the potential for higher returns compared to regular savings accounts.

There are many different types of investments, each with its own risks and rewards. Stocks are shares of ownership in a company. When you buy a stock, you become a part-owner of that company and can earn money through dividends and capital gains. Bonds are loans you make to a company or government. In return, they pay you interest over a set period of time. Mutual funds and ETFs (exchange-traded funds) are collections of stocks and bonds that you can buy as a single investment. They offer diversification and professional management.

Real estate is another type of investment. This involves buying property, like a house or an apartment, and renting it out or selling it for a profit. Real estate can provide a steady income and potential for appreciation, but it also comes with risks and responsibilities.

Starting with small investments can help you get comfortable with investing. You don't need a lot of money to start investing. Many online platforms and apps allow you to start with just a few dollars. The key is to start early and be consistent.

Risk and reward are important concepts in investing. Generally, higher-risk investments have the potential for higher returns, but they also come with a greater chance of losing money. Lower-risk investments are safer but usually offer lower returns. It's important to find a balance that fits your risk tolerance and financial goals.

Diversification is a strategy to reduce risk by spreading your money across different types of investments. By diversifying your investments, you can protect yourself from losses if one investment performs poorly. This is why mutual funds and ETFs can be a good option for beginners.

Creating an investment plan is crucial for success. This involves setting clear goals, determining your risk tolerance, and choosing the right investments to achieve those goals. Your plan should be tailored to your individual needs and circumstances.

Understanding the stock market is essential for investing in stocks. The stock market is where stocks are bought and sold. Prices can fluctuate based on supply and demand, company performance, and economic factors. Learning how the stock market works can help you make informed investment decisions.

Buying and selling stocks can be done through a brokerage account. A broker is a person or company that buys and sells stocks on your behalf. There are many online brokers that offer low fees and user-friendly platforms. When choosing a broker, consider factors like fees, account minimums, and the types of investments they offer.

Reading stock charts can help you analyze the performance of a stock. Stock charts show the price history of a stock over time, along with other information like volume and moving averages. By understanding stock charts, you can make better decisions about when to buy or sell.

Investment strategies can vary based on your goals and risk tolerance. Some common strategies include buy and hold, which involves buying stocks and holding them for a long time, and dollar-cost averaging, which involves investing a fixed amount of money at regular intervals. Both strategies can help you build wealth over time.

Long-term vs. short-term investing is another consideration. Long-term investing involves holding investments for several years or even decades, while short-term investing involves buying and selling within a shorter period. Long-term investing is generally less risky and can provide more stable returns.

Compound interest is a powerful concept in investing. This is when the interest you earn on an investment is reinvested, so you earn interest on both your original investment and the interest. Over time, this can significantly increase the value of your investments.

Dividends are payments made by a company to its shareholders, usually from its profits. Not all stocks pay dividends, but those that do can provide a steady income. Reinvesting dividends can help your investments grow even faster.

Tax implications are an important consideration when investing. Different types of investments have different tax treatments. For example, capital gains from selling stocks are usually taxed at a lower rate than regular income. It's important to understand the tax implications of your investments and consider strategies to minimize your tax bill.

Retirement accounts, like 401(k) plans and IRAs, are tax-advantaged accounts designed to help you save for retirement. Contributions to these accounts are often tax-deductible, and the money grows tax-free until you withdraw it in retirement. Taking advantage of retirement accounts can help you save more for the future.

Choosing the right investments can be challenging, but it's important to do your research and seek professional advice if needed. Consider factors like your financial goals, risk tolerance, and investment time horizon when making investment decisions.

Avoiding common investment mistakes can help you succeed. Some common mistakes include trying to time the market, chasing high returns, and not diversifying your investments. By staying informed and sticking to your investment plan, you can avoid these pitfalls.

Financial advisors can provide valuable guidance and support. They can help you create an investment plan, choose the right investments, and stay on track with your goals. When choosing a financial advisor, look for someone with experience, credentials, and a good track record.

In summary, investing for beginners doesn't have to be intimidating. By understanding the basics, creating a plan, and making informed decisions, you can grow your money and achieve your financial goals. This chapter has provided a foundation to help you get started on your investing journey.

Chapter 6: Planning for Retirement

Retirement planning is an essential part of personal finance. While it may seem far off, the earlier you start planning for retirement, the better prepared you'll be. This chapter will guide you through the basics of retirement planning and help you create a plan to ensure a comfortable and secure retirement.

One of the first steps in retirement planning is understanding the importance of saving for retirement. During retirement, you'll need enough money to cover your living expenses, healthcare costs, and any other needs or wants you may have. Without a steady income from work, your savings and investments will be your primary source of funds.

When to start planning for retirement is a common question. The answer is as soon as possible. The earlier you start saving, the more time your money has to grow through compound interest. Even small contributions made early on can add up to a significant amount over time.

Setting retirement goals is a crucial part of the planning process. Think about what you want your retirement to look like. Do you plan to travel, pursue hobbies, or spend more time with family? Estimating your future expenses can help you determine how much you'll need to save.

How much to save for retirement depends on various factors, including your desired lifestyle, expected expenses, and life expectancy. A common rule of thumb is to aim to replace 70-80% of your pre-retirement income. However, your specific needs may vary, so it's important to create a personalized plan.

There are different types of retirement accounts designed to help you save for the future. A 401(k) plan is an employer-sponsored retirement account that allows you to contribute a portion of your salary, often with employer matching. Individual Retirement Accounts (IRAs) are another option, available to anyone with earned income.

Roth IRA vs. traditional IRA is a decision many people face. With a traditional IRA, contributions are tax-deductible, and the money grows tax-deferred until you withdraw it in retirement. With a Roth IRA, contributions are made with after-tax dollars, but withdrawals in retirement are tax-free. Both options have their benefits, so choose the one that best fits your situation.

Employer-sponsored retirement plans, like 401(k) plans, often come with benefits like employer matching and automatic payroll deductions. Take full advantage of these benefits to maximize your retirement savings. If your employer offers a matching contribution, try to contribute at least enough to get the full match.

Understanding Social Security is an important part of retirement planning. Social Security provides a source of income for retirees, but it may not be enough to cover all your expenses. Estimate your future Social Security benefits and consider them as part of your overall retirement plan.

Pensions and annuities are other sources of retirement income. A pension is a retirement plan that provides a fixed monthly income, usually based on your years of service and salary. Annuities are insurance products that provide a guaranteed income stream for a certain period or for life. Both can provide additional financial security in retirement.

Maximizing retirement benefits involves making strategic decisions about when to start collecting benefits and how to manage your retirement accounts. For example, delaying Social Security benefits can increase your monthly payments. Similarly, making catch-up contributions to your retirement accounts if you're over 50 can boost your savings.

Retirement savings strategies can vary, but some common ones include contributing regularly to retirement accounts, taking advantage of employer matching, and investing in a diversified portfolio. Staying disciplined and consistent with your savings can help you build a substantial retirement nest egg.

Catch-up contributions allow people aged 50 and older to contribute more to their retirement accounts. This can help you make up for any lost time or increase your savings as you approach retirement. Take advantage of these opportunities to boost your retirement savings.

Tax benefits of retirement accounts are another important consideration. Contributions to traditional IRAs and 401(k) plans are often tax-deductible, reducing your taxable income. The money in these accounts grows tax-deferred until you withdraw it in retirement. Understanding the tax benefits can help you make informed decisions about your retirement savings.

Investment options for retirement include stocks, bonds, mutual funds, and real estate. A diversified investment portfolio can help you balance risk and reward, providing growth potential while protecting your savings from market volatility. Consider your risk tolerance and investment time horizon when choosing investments.

Diversifying retirement investments is crucial for managing risk. By spreading your money across different types of investments, you can reduce the impact of poor performance in any one area. Diversification can help you achieve more stable and consistent returns over time.

Managing retirement income is an important part of retirement planning. Once you retire, you'll need to create a plan for withdrawing money from your retirement accounts. This may involve setting a withdrawal rate, considering tax implications, and making adjustments based on your needs and market conditions.

Planning for healthcare costs is another essential aspect of retirement planning. Healthcare expenses can be significant in retirement, so it's important to include them in your budget. Consider options like Medicare, supplemental insurance, and health savings accounts (HSAs) to help cover these costs.

Estate planning is also important for retirement. This involves creating a will, establishing trusts, and making arrangements for the distribution of your assets after your death. Proper estate planning can ensure that your wishes are carried out and provide financial security for your loved ones.

Creating a will and trust is a key part of estate planning. A will is a legal document that outlines how you want your assets distributed after your death. A trust can help manage your assets during your lifetime and after your death, providing more control and potentially reducing taxes.

Power of attorney and healthcare directives are important documents to have in place. A power of attorney allows someone to make financial decisions on your behalf if you're unable to do so. Healthcare directives outline your wishes for medical care in case you become incapacitated.

Planning for unexpected expenses is crucial in retirement. No matter how carefully you plan, there will always be unforeseen costs. Having a financial cushion and being prepared can help you handle these situations without derailing your retirement plan.

Enjoying retirement is the ultimate goal. After years of hard work, you deserve to enjoy your retirement years. Plan activities and hobbies that bring you joy and fulfillment. Staying active and engaged can help you maintain a healthy and happy retirement.

This chapter has provided an overview of retirement planning and the steps you can take to ensure a comfortable and secure retirement. By starting early, setting goals, and making informed decisions, you can build a retirement plan that meets your needs and allows you to enjoy your golden years.

Chapter 7: Protecting Your Finances

Protecting your finances is an essential part of personal finance. Life is unpredictable, and having the right protections in place can help you weather financial storms and keep your money safe. This chapter will cover various ways to protect your finances, from insurance to identity theft prevention.

Insurance is one of the primary tools for financial protection. It provides a safety net in case of unexpected events, like illness, accidents, or natural disasters. There are many types of insurance, each designed to protect different aspects of your life and finances.

Health insurance is crucial for covering medical expenses. Without it, a serious illness or injury could result in significant financial hardship. Health insurance helps pay for doctor visits, hospital stays, and prescription medications. Make sure you have adequate coverage to protect yourself and your family.

Life insurance is another important type of insurance. It provides financial support to your loved ones in the event of your death. There are different types of life insurance, including term life and whole life. Term life insurance provides coverage for a specific period, while whole life insurance provides coverage for your entire life.

Disability insurance protects your income if you become unable to work due to illness or injury. This type of insurance can help cover your living expenses and maintain your financial stability during a difficult time. Consider both short-term and long-term disability insurance to ensure comprehensive protection.

Homeowners and renters insurance protect your property and belongings. Homeowners insurance covers damage to your home and its contents, as well as liability for accidents that occur on your property. Renters insurance covers your personal belongings if you rent your home. Both types of insurance provide valuable protection against loss or damage.

Auto insurance is required by law in most places and protects you financially in case of a car accident. It covers damage to your vehicle, medical expenses, and liability for injuries or damage to others. Make sure you have adequate coverage to protect yourself and your assets.

Travel insurance can provide peace of mind when you're away from home. It covers unexpected events like trip cancellations, medical emergencies, and lost luggage. If you travel frequently, consider getting a travel insurance policy to protect yourself and your belongings.

Pet insurance can help cover the cost of veterinary care for your pets. Pets are part of the family, and their medical expenses can add up quickly. Pet insurance can help you afford necessary treatments and keep your furry friends healthy.

Choosing the right insurance policies involves considering your needs and budget. Compare different policies and providers to find the best coverage at the best price. Don't skimp on insurance; having adequate coverage can save you a lot of money and stress in the long run.

An emergency fund is another important financial protection. This is a savings account set aside for unexpected expenses, like car repairs, medical bills, or job loss. Having an emergency fund can help you avoid debt and maintain financial stability during tough times.

Identity theft protection is becoming increasingly important in today's digital world. Identity theft occurs when someone steals your personal information and uses it to commit fraud. Protect yourself by using strong passwords, monitoring your accounts, and being cautious with your personal information.

Avoiding scams and fraud is also crucial. Scammers are constantly coming up with new ways to trick people out of their money. Be skeptical of unsolicited offers, never give out your personal information to unknown sources, and report any suspicious activity.

Safe online banking practices can help protect your finances. Use secure passwords, enable two-factor authentication, and monitor your accounts regularly for any unauthorized transactions. Be cautious when using public Wi-Fi and only access your accounts from secure devices.

Keeping financial information secure involves safeguarding documents like bank statements, tax returns, and insurance policies. Store important documents in a safe place and shred any sensitive information before disposing of it. Consider using a safe deposit box for valuable items.

Financial literacy is an important aspect of protecting your finances. The more you know about personal finance, the better equipped you'll be to make smart decisions and avoid pitfalls. Continuously educate yourself about money management and stay informed about financial news and trends.

Teaching kids about money is another way to protect your family's finances. By instilling good financial habits in your children, you can help them avoid common mistakes and build a strong financial future. Use everyday opportunities to teach them about saving, budgeting, and making wise financial choices.

Financial planning for life changes is crucial for maintaining stability. Major events like getting married, having a baby, or changing jobs can significantly impact your finances. Plan ahead for these changes and adjust your financial strategies as needed to stay on track.

Protecting family assets through diversification is a smart strategy. By spreading your investments across different asset classes, you can reduce risk and increase the potential for returns. This can help protect your family's wealth and provide financial security for the future.

Regular financial checkups are important for keeping your finances on track. Review your budget, savings, and investments periodically to ensure they still align with your goals. Make adjustments as needed to stay on course and protect your financial health.

Handling financial setbacks with resilience is key to long-term success. No matter how well you plan, there will always be unexpected challenges. Stay positive, focus on solutions, and seek support if needed. Resilience and adaptability can help you overcome setbacks and emerge stronger.

Seeking professional advice can provide valuable insights and guidance. Financial advisors, insurance agents, and other professionals can help you make informed decisions and protect your finances. Don't hesitate to reach out for help when needed.

In summary, protecting your finances involves a combination of insurance, emergency savings, financial literacy, and smart planning. By taking these steps, you can safeguard your money, reduce stress, and ensure a secure financial future for yourself and your family.

Chapter 8: Taxes Made Simple

Taxes are a part of life, and understanding how they work can help you manage your finances more effectively. While taxes might seem complicated, this chapter will break them down into simple, easy-to-understand concepts. By the end of this chapter, you'll have a better grasp of how taxes affect your finances and how to make smart tax decisions.

Taxes are payments we make to the government to fund public services like schools, roads, and healthcare. There are many different types of taxes, including income tax, sales tax, property tax, and more. Each type of tax serves a different purpose and is calculated in a different way.

Income tax is one of the most common types of taxes. It's a tax on the money you earn from work, investments, and other sources. The amount of income tax you pay depends on your income level and the tax rates set by the government. Income tax is usually withheld from your paycheck by your employer and sent to the government on your behalf.

Filing a tax return is how you report your income and taxes paid to the government. In the United States, most people file their tax returns each year by April 15th. Your tax return shows how much money you earned, how much tax was withheld, and any deductions or credits you qualify for. If you paid too much tax, you'll get a refund; if you didn't pay enough, you'll owe additional tax.

Tax brackets and rates determine how much tax you owe based on your income. The tax system is progressive, meaning that higher income levels are taxed at higher rates. For example, if your income falls into the lowest tax bracket, you'll pay a lower rate on that portion of your income, while higher income portions will be taxed at higher rates.

Tax deductions and credits can help reduce your tax bill. Deductions lower your taxable income, which means you pay less tax. Common deductions include mortgage interest, student loan interest, and charitable donations. Tax credits, on the other hand, directly reduce the amount of tax you owe. Some credits, like the Earned Income Tax Credit, can even result in a refund if you owe no tax.

The standard deduction is a set amount that you can subtract from your income if you don't itemize your deductions. Itemizing involves listing specific expenses that qualify as deductions. Most people choose the option that gives them the largest deduction. The standard deduction amount varies based on your filing status, such as single, married filing jointly, or head of household.

Reducing your tax bill involves taking advantage of deductions, credits, and other tax benefits. Contributing to retirement accounts, like a 401(k) or IRA, can lower your taxable income and provide future financial security. Making charitable donations, paying for education expenses, and claiming dependent care credits can also help reduce your tax bill.

Tax-advantaged accounts are designed to help you save for specific goals while providing tax benefits. Retirement accounts, like 401(k) plans and IRAs, offer tax-deferred growth, meaning you don't pay taxes on the money until you withdraw it in retirement. Health Savings Accounts (HSAs) and Education Savings Accounts (ESAs) also offer tax advantages for medical and education expenses.

The tax implications of investments are important to understand. When you sell an investment for a profit, you may owe capital gains tax. The tax rate on capital gains depends on how long you held the investment and your income level. Investments held for more than a year are subject to lower long-term capital gains rates, while those held for a shorter period are taxed at higher short-term rates.

Retirement account taxes can impact your savings. Traditional retirement accounts, like 401(k) plans and traditional IRAs, offer tax-deferred growth, but you'll owe taxes on withdrawals in retirement. Roth IRAs, on the other hand, are funded with after-tax dollars, so withdrawals in retirement are tax-free. Understanding these differences can help you make informed decisions about your retirement savings.

Estate and gift taxes apply to the transfer of wealth. Estate tax is a tax on the value of your estate (your property and assets) when you die. Gift tax applies to large gifts you give during your lifetime. Both taxes have exemptions, meaning you can transfer a certain amount of money tax-free. Proper estate planning can help you minimize these taxes and ensure your assets go to your intended beneficiaries.

Self-employment taxes are another consideration if you run your own business or work as a freelancer. Self-employed individuals must pay both the employee and employer portions of Social Security and Medicare taxes. This can be a significant expense, so it's important to plan for these taxes and set aside money to cover them.

Small business taxes can be complex, involving income tax, payroll tax, sales tax, and more. Keeping good records, understanding your tax obligations, and working with a tax professional can help you manage your business taxes effectively.

Sales tax is a tax on goods and services you purchase. The rate varies by state and locality. Some items, like groceries and medicine, may be exempt from sales tax or taxed at a lower rate. Understanding sales tax can help you budget for your purchases and avoid surprises at the checkout.

Property taxes are taxes on real estate, like your home or land. The amount you pay is based on the assessed value of your property and the tax rate set by your local government. Property taxes fund local services like schools, police, and fire departments. If you own property, it's important to budget for property taxes and understand how they're calculated.

Avoiding tax penalties is crucial for managing your finances. Penalties can apply if you don't pay your taxes on time, underreport your income, or fail to file a tax return. To avoid penalties, make sure to file your tax return by the deadline, pay any taxes owed, and keep accurate records of your income and expenses.

Keeping good records is essential for tax purposes. Save documents like pay stubs, bank statements, receipts, and tax forms. Organized records can make filing your tax return easier and help you claim all the deductions and credits you're entitled to. In case of an audit, good records can also help you prove the accuracy of your return.

Using tax software can simplify the process of filing your tax return. Many software programs guide you through the process, ask questions about your income and expenses, and help you find deductions and credits. Some programs even offer free filing for simple returns. Choose a reputable tax software that meets your needs.

Working with a tax professional can provide valuable insights and ensure your taxes are done correctly. A tax professional can help you navigate complex tax situations, find tax-saving opportunities, and represent you in case of an audit. When choosing a tax professional, look for someone with experience, credentials, and a good reputation.

Tax planning strategies can help you manage your tax bill and achieve your financial goals. This might include timing your income and expenses to take advantage of lower tax rates, maximizing deductions and credits, and using tax-advantaged accounts. Regularly reviewing your tax situation and making adjustments as needed can help you stay on track.

Understanding taxes is an important part of managing your finances. By knowing how taxes work and taking advantage of tax benefits, you can reduce your tax bill and keep more of your hard-earned money. This chapter has provided an overview of the key concepts and strategies to help you navigate the world of taxes with confidence.

Chapter 9: Building Wealth

Building wealth is a long-term goal that requires planning, discipline, and smart financial decisions. Wealth isn't just about having a lot of money; it's about creating financial security and freedom. This chapter will guide you through the steps to build wealth and achieve your financial goals.

Wealth is different from income. Income is the money you earn from work, investments, or other sources. Wealth, on the other hand, is the accumulation of assets, like savings, investments, and property, minus any debts. Building wealth involves increasing your assets and reducing your liabilities.

One of the first steps to building wealth is setting clear financial goals. Think about what you want to achieve, whether it's buying a house, saving for retirement, or starting a business. Having specific, measurable goals can help you stay focused and motivated.

The power of compound interest is a key concept in wealth building. Compound interest is when the interest you earn on your savings or investments is reinvested, so you earn interest on both your original amount and the interest. Over time, this can significantly increase the value of your investments.

Saving vs. investing is an important distinction. Saving is setting aside money for short-term needs or emergencies, while investing is putting your money into assets with the potential for growth over the long term. Both are important for building wealth, but investing can help your money grow faster.

Passive income streams can boost your wealth-building efforts. Passive income is money you earn with little to no effort, like rental income, dividends from investments, or royalties from a book or invention. Developing passive income streams can provide additional financial security and help you achieve your goals faster.

Real estate investing is a popular way to build wealth. This involves buying property, like a house or apartment, and renting it out or selling it for a profit.

Real estate can provide a steady income and potential for appreciation, but it also comes with risks and responsibilities.

Starting a business can be a path to wealth. Owning your own business allows you to control your income and build equity. However, starting and running a business requires hard work, dedication, and smart financial management. If you have an entrepreneurial spirit, this can be a rewarding way to build wealth.

Diversifying income sources is another strategy for building wealth. Relying on a single source of income can be risky. By having multiple income streams, like a job, investments, and side hustles, you can increase your financial stability and growth potential.

Increasing your income is a key part of building wealth. Look for opportunities to advance in your career, take on additional work, or develop new skills. Higher income can provide more money to save and invest, accelerating your wealth-building efforts.

Side hustles and part-time jobs can provide extra income. A side hustle is a small business or gig you do in addition to your main job, like freelancing, tutoring, or selling handmade crafts. This extra income can help you reach your financial goals faster.

Monetizing hobbies and skills is another way to boost your income. Think about what you enjoy doing and how you can turn it into a source of income. This might include teaching a class, writing a blog, or selling your artwork. Doing something you love can make earning extra money more enjoyable.

Creating multiple income streams can help you build wealth faster. By diversifying your income, you can reduce risk and increase your financial stability. This might include having a job, investments, a side hustle, and rental income. The more income streams you have, the more secure your financial situation will be.

Building wealth through stocks involves investing in shares of companies. Stocks can provide high returns, but they also come with risk. It's important to do your research, diversify your investments, and be prepared for market fluctuations. Over the long term, stocks can be a powerful tool for building wealth.

Bonds are another investment option for wealth building. Bonds are loans you make to a company or government in exchange for interest payments. They are generally less risky than stocks and can provide steady income. Including bonds in your investment portfolio can help balance risk and reward.

Mutual funds and ETFs are collections of stocks and bonds that you can buy as a single investment. They offer diversification and professional management, making them a good option for beginners. By investing in mutual funds or ETFs, you can spread your risk and potentially achieve higher returns.

Retirement accounts, like 401(k) plans and IRAs, are important for building long-term wealth. Contributions to these accounts are often tax-deductible, and the money grows tax-free until you withdraw it in retirement. Taking advantage of retirement accounts can help you save more and build wealth over time.

Using tax strategies to build wealth involves taking advantage of tax benefits and minimizing your tax bill. This might include contributing to tax-advantaged accounts, claiming deductions and credits, and timing your income and expenses to reduce taxes. Understanding the tax implications of your financial decisions can help you build wealth more effectively.

Financial education is crucial for building wealth. The more you know about personal finance, investing, and money management, the better equipped you'll be to make smart financial decisions. Continuously educate yourself and stay informed about financial news and trends.

Avoiding lifestyle inflation is important for building wealth. Lifestyle inflation occurs when your spending increases as your income increases. While it's natural to want to enjoy the fruits of your labor, it's important to keep your spending in check and prioritize saving and investing.

Staying disciplined with money is key to achieving your wealth-building goals. This means sticking to your budget, avoiding unnecessary spending, and making consistent contributions to your savings and investments. Discipline and consistency are essential for long-term financial success.

Building wealth over time requires patience and perseverance. Wealth doesn't happen overnight; it's the result of making smart financial decisions and sticking to your plan. Stay focused on your goals, adjust your strategies as needed, and celebrate your progress along the way.

Celebrating wealth milestones can help you stay motivated. Set smaller goals along the way and celebrate when you reach them. This can make the journey to building wealth more enjoyable and rewarding.

In summary, building wealth is about creating financial security and freedom. By setting goals, saving, investing, and making smart financial decisions, you can increase your assets and achieve your financial dreams. This chapter has provided a roadmap to help you start building wealth today.

Chapter 10: Financial Planning for Families

Financial planning for families is essential for ensuring financial stability and achieving long-term goals. Whether you're planning for your child's education, buying a home, or preparing for retirement, having a solid financial plan can help you navigate the challenges and opportunities of family life. This chapter will guide you through the key aspects of family financial planning.

Setting family financial goals is the first step in creating a financial plan. Discuss with your family what you want to achieve, both in the short term and the long term. This might include saving for a vacation, paying off debt, or building an emergency fund. Having clear, shared goals can help you stay focused and work together towards achieving them.

Creating a family budget is crucial for managing your finances. A budget helps you track your income and expenses, so you know exactly where your money is going. Start by listing all sources of income, like salaries, bonuses, and investment earnings. Then, list your expenses, including fixed costs like rent or mortgage payments, and variable costs like groceries and entertainment.

Teaching kids about money is an important part of family financial planning. By instilling good financial habits in your children, you can help them avoid common mistakes and build a strong financial future. Use everyday opportunities to teach them about saving, budgeting, and making wise financial choices.

Saving for your children's education is a significant goal for many families. Education can be expensive, but starting early can help reduce the financial burden. Consider setting up an education savings account, like a 529 plan, to save for college. These accounts offer tax advantages and can help you build a substantial fund over time.

Managing family expenses involves balancing the needs and wants of all family members. It's important to prioritize essential expenses, like housing, food, and healthcare, while also making room for discretionary spending, like vacations and hobbies. Communication and compromise are key to managing family finances effectively.

Handling family financial emergencies is another important aspect of planning. An emergency fund is a savings account set aside for unexpected expenses, like car repairs, medical bills, or job loss. Aim to save enough to cover three to six months of living expenses. Having an emergency fund can provide peace of mind and financial stability during tough times.

Protecting family assets is crucial for maintaining financial security. This includes having adequate insurance coverage, like health, life, and homeowners insurance. Insurance can help protect your family from financial hardship in case of illness, accident, or loss. Review your insurance policies regularly to ensure you have the right coverage for your needs.

Planning for family vacations involves budgeting and saving. Decide on a vacation destination and estimate the costs, including travel, accommodation, food, and activities. Create a savings plan to set aside money for the trip. This can help you avoid going into debt and ensure you have a fun and relaxing vacation.

Budgeting for holidays and celebrations is another important consideration. Holidays and special occasions can be expensive, but with careful planning, you can enjoy them without breaking the bank. Set a budget for gifts, decorations, and entertainment, and look for ways to save, like DIY projects or shopping sales.

Managing debt as a family involves working together to pay off any outstanding debts. This might include credit card debt, student loans, or a mortgage. Create a plan to pay off your debts, starting with the highest-interest debts first. Communicate openly about your progress and celebrate your successes along the way.

Building a family emergency fund provides a financial safety net for unexpected expenses. An emergency fund can help you avoid going into debt and maintain financial stability during tough times. Aim to save enough to cover three to six months of living expenses. Regularly contribute to your emergency fund and review your savings goals as your family's needs change.

Planning for family health expenses is crucial for maintaining financial stability. Healthcare costs can be significant, so it's important to include them in your budget. Consider options like health savings accounts (HSAs) or flexible spending accounts (FSAs) to help cover medical expenses. Review your health insurance coverage regularly to ensure it meets your family's needs.

Estate planning for families involves creating a plan for the distribution of your assets after your death. This includes creating a will, establishing trusts, and making arrangements for the care of your children. Proper estate planning can ensure that your wishes are carried out and provide financial security for your loved ones.

Creating a family financial plan involves setting goals, creating a budget, and developing strategies to achieve those goals. Regularly review and update your plan to ensure it still aligns with your family's needs and circumstances. Involve all family members in the planning process to ensure everyone is on the same page.

Financial communication is key to successful family financial planning. Discuss your goals, budget, and progress regularly with your family. Open and honest communication can help prevent misunderstandings and ensure everyone is working towards the same goals.

Involving kids in budgeting can teach them valuable financial skills and help them understand the importance of managing money. Encourage them to set their own savings goals, track their spending, and make smart financial choices. Use tools like allowance or chore charts to help them learn about earning and saving money.

Teaching teens about credit is important for helping them build a strong financial future. Explain how credit works, including the importance of paying bills on time, keeping balances low, and avoiding unnecessary debt. Consider giving them a credit card with a low limit to help them learn how to use credit responsibly.

Planning for family milestones, like weddings, graduations, and retirements, involves budgeting and saving. Estimate the costs of these events and create a

MASTERING MONEY: A FUN GUIDE TO PERSONAL FINANCE

savings plan to cover them. This can help you avoid financial stress and ensure you can celebrate these important moments without going into debt.

The importance of financial literacy for kids cannot be overstated. Teaching your children about money management from a young age can set them up for a lifetime of financial success. Use everyday opportunities to teach them about saving, budgeting, and making wise financial choices.

Building a legacy for your family involves creating a plan for the future. This might include setting up trusts, making charitable donations, or passing on family businesses or property. Proper planning can ensure your assets are used in a way that aligns with your values and provides for your loved ones.

Seeking professional advice for family finances can provide valuable insights and guidance. Financial advisors, insurance agents, and other professionals can help you make informed decisions and protect your family's financial future. Don't hesitate to reach out for help when needed.

In summary, financial planning for families involves setting goals, creating a budget, and developing strategies to achieve those goals. By working together, communicating openly, and seeking professional advice, you can ensure financial stability and security for your family.

Chapter 11: Navigating Major Life Events

Major life events can have a significant impact on your finances. Whether you're getting married, buying a home, or starting a family, it's important to plan ahead and make informed financial decisions. This chapter will guide you through the financial aspects of navigating major life events and help you stay on track with your goals.

Getting married is an exciting milestone, but it also comes with financial implications. Combining finances with your spouse requires open communication and planning. Discuss your financial goals, create a joint budget, and decide how you'll handle expenses and savings. Consider setting up a joint bank account for shared expenses while keeping individual accounts for personal spending.

Buying a home is one of the biggest financial decisions you'll make. It's important to assess your financial situation and determine how much you can afford. Save for a down payment, get pre-approved for a mortgage, and shop around for the best loan terms. Don't forget to budget for additional costs like property taxes, insurance, and maintenance.

Starting a family involves planning for the financial costs of raising children. This includes healthcare, childcare, education, and everyday expenses. Create a budget to account for these costs and start saving early. Consider setting up a college savings account, like a 529 plan, to help cover future education expenses.

Saving for kids' education is a significant goal for many families. Education can be expensive, but starting early can help reduce the financial burden. Look into education savings accounts, like a 529 plan, to save for college. These accounts offer tax advantages and can help you build a substantial fund over time.

Dealing with job loss is a challenging situation that can impact your finances. If you lose your job, it's important to review your budget, cut unnecessary expenses, and focus on finding new employment. An emergency fund can provide a financial cushion during this time and help you cover essential expenses.

Handling a divorce involves navigating the financial aspects of splitting assets and managing expenses. Work with a financial advisor or attorney to ensure a fair division of property and debts. Update your budget, review your insurance coverage, and create a new financial plan to reflect your changed circumstances.

Financial impacts of illness or disability can be significant. It's important to have adequate health and disability insurance to cover medical expenses and protect your income. Create an emergency fund to help cover unexpected costs and review your budget to ensure it accommodates any changes in your financial situation.

Planning for retirement involves saving and investing for your future. The earlier you start, the more time your money has to grow. Contribute to retirement accounts like a 401(k) or IRA, take advantage of employer matching, and diversify your investments. Regularly review your retirement plan and make adjustments as needed.

Caring for aging parents can be both emotionally and financially challenging. Discuss your parents' financial situation, healthcare needs, and long-term care options. Create a plan to cover costs and consider options like long-term care insurance or government assistance programs. Communicate openly with your family to ensure everyone is on the same page.

Managing inheritance involves making informed decisions about how to use the money you receive. Consider paying off debt, saving for future goals, or investing to grow your wealth. Work with a financial advisor to create a plan that aligns with your goals and values.

Planning for major purchases, like a car or home renovation, requires budgeting and saving. Estimate the costs, create a savings plan, and look for ways to reduce expenses. Consider financing options and compare interest rates to find the best deal.

Moving and relocation costs can add up quickly. Create a budget to cover moving expenses, including packing supplies, transportation, and new furnishings. Look for ways to save, like decluttering before you move and shopping for deals on moving services.

Starting a business is an exciting but challenging endeavor. It requires careful planning and financial management. Create a business plan, secure funding, and keep detailed records of your income and expenses. Be prepared for the financial ups and downs of entrepreneurship and seek professional advice when needed.

Dealing with financial windfalls, like a bonus or inheritance, requires careful planning. It's important to make thoughtful decisions about how to use the money. Consider paying off debt, saving for future goals, or investing to grow your wealth. Work with a financial advisor to create a plan that aligns with your goals and values.

Preparing for natural disasters involves creating a plan to protect your finances and property. This might include having adequate insurance coverage, creating an emergency fund, and keeping important documents in a safe place. Being prepared can help you recover more quickly and reduce the financial impact of a disaster.

Handling unexpected expenses is a crucial part of financial planning. No matter how carefully you plan, there will always be unforeseen costs. Having an emergency fund can help you cover these expenses without derailing your financial goals. Regularly review and adjust your budget to accommodate any changes in your financial situation.

Financial impacts of legal issues, like lawsuits or divorce, can be significant. It's important to seek professional advice and create a plan to manage these costs. Review your budget, insurance coverage, and financial goals to ensure you can handle any financial challenges that arise.

Planning for career changes involves assessing your financial situation and creating a plan to achieve your goals. This might include saving for additional education, building an emergency fund, or adjusting your budget to reflect changes in your income. Be prepared for the financial ups and downs of changing careers and stay focused on your long-term goals.

Adjusting to changes in income requires flexibility and planning. Whether your income increases or decreases, it's important to review your budget, adjust your savings goals, and make informed financial decisions. Stay focused on your long-term goals and be prepared to make adjustments as needed.

Managing financial stress is important for your overall well-being. Major life events can be stressful, but having a solid financial plan can help you stay focused and reduce anxiety. Practice self-care, seek support from friends and family, and consider working with a financial advisor to help you navigate financial challenges.

Resilience is key to navigating major life events. No matter how well you plan, there will always be unexpected challenges. Stay positive, focus on solutions, and seek support if needed. Resilience and adaptability can help you overcome setbacks and emerge stronger.

Seeking support and advice can provide valuable insights and guidance. Financial advisors, counselors, and other professionals can help you make informed decisions and navigate major life events. Don't hesitate to reach out for help when needed.

This chapter has provided an overview of the financial aspects of navigating major life events. By planning ahead, making informed decisions, and seeking support when needed, you can manage the financial challenges and opportunities that come with life's milestones.

Chapter 12: Financial Freedom and Independence

Financial freedom is the ultimate goal for many people. It means having enough money to live the life you want without financial stress or constraints. Achieving financial freedom requires planning, discipline, and smart financial decisions. This chapter will guide you through the steps to achieve financial independence and enjoy the benefits of financial freedom.

Financial freedom means different things to different people. For some, it might mean retiring early, while for others, it might mean having enough money to travel or pursue hobbies. Whatever your definition, the key is to set clear goals and create a plan to achieve them.

Steps to achieve financial independence involve saving, investing, and managing your money wisely. Start by setting specific, measurable goals and creating a budget to track your income and expenses. Focus on saving a portion of your income each month and investing it to grow your wealth.

Setting financial freedom goals is crucial for staying focused and motivated. Think about what you want your life to look like and how much money you'll need to achieve it. Break your goals down into smaller, manageable steps and create a plan to reach them.

Building passive income is a key part of achieving financial independence. Passive income is money you earn with little to no effort, like rental income, dividends from investments, or royalties from a book or invention. Developing passive income streams can provide additional financial security and help you achieve your goals faster.

Frugality is about being mindful of your spending and looking for ways to save money. This doesn't mean being cheap or depriving yourself, but rather making thoughtful choices about how you spend your money. By living below your means, you can save more and build wealth faster.

Saving aggressively is another strategy for achieving financial independence. This means setting aside a larger portion of your income for savings and investments. The more you save, the faster you can achieve your financial goals. Look for ways to cut unnecessary expenses and increase your savings rate.

Investing for the long term is crucial for building wealth. Investing your money can help it grow faster than just saving it in a bank. Focus on a diversified investment portfolio that includes stocks, bonds, and other assets. Stay disciplined and avoid trying to time the market.

The power of compound interest is a key concept in achieving financial independence. Compound interest is when the interest you earn on your savings or investments is reinvested, so you earn interest on both your original amount and the interest. Over time, this can significantly increase the value of your investments.

Reducing and eliminating debt is important for financial freedom. Debt can be a major obstacle to achieving your goals, so focus on paying off any outstanding debts as quickly as possible. Use strategies like the snowball or avalanche method to tackle your debts and stay motivated.

Maximizing income is a key part of achieving financial independence. Look for opportunities to advance in your career, take on additional work, or develop new skills. Higher income can provide more money to save and invest, accelerating your wealth-building efforts.

Diversifying investments is crucial for managing risk. By spreading your money across different types of investments, you can reduce the impact of poor performance in any one area. Diversification can help you achieve more stable and consistent returns over time.

Creating a financial independence plan involves setting goals, creating a budget, and developing strategies to achieve those goals. Regularly review and update your plan to ensure it still aligns with your needs and circumstances. Stay focused on your goals and be prepared to make adjustments as needed.

Financial literacy is essential for achieving financial independence. The more you know about personal finance, investing, and money management, the better equipped you'll be to make smart financial decisions. Continuously educate yourself and stay informed about financial news and trends.

Staying motivated on the journey to financial independence can be challenging, but it's important to stay focused on your goals. Celebrate your successes along the way and remind yourself of the benefits of financial freedom. Surround yourself with like-minded people who support your goals.

Avoiding lifestyle inflation is important for achieving financial independence. Lifestyle inflation occurs when your spending increases as your income increases. While it's natural to want to enjoy the fruits of your labor, it's important to keep your spending in check and prioritize saving and investing.

Building a financial cushion provides a safety net for unexpected expenses. An emergency fund can help you cover unexpected costs without derailing your financial goals. Aim to save enough to cover three to six months of living expenses. Regularly contribute to your emergency fund and review your savings goals as your needs change.

Planning for early retirement is a common goal for many seeking financial independence. To achieve this, you'll need to save and invest aggressively, reduce your expenses, and create a plan for managing your money in retirement. Consider factors like healthcare costs, inflation, and how you'll generate income in retirement.

Living below your means is a fundamental principle of financial independence. This means spending less than you earn and avoiding debt. It can be tempting to buy things you can't afford, but living below your means will help you build financial security and avoid stress.

Staying disciplined with money is key to achieving your financial goals. This means sticking to your budget, avoiding unnecessary spending, and making consistent contributions to your savings and investments. Discipline and consistency are essential for long-term financial success.

Celebrating financial milestones can help you stay motivated. Set smaller goals along the way and celebrate when you reach them. This can make the journey to financial independence more enjoyable and rewarding.

Staying focused on goals is crucial for achieving financial independence. Life is full of distractions, but staying focused on your goals can help you stay on track. Regularly review your progress, adjust your plan as needed, and stay committed to your financial journey.

Seeking support from like-minded people can provide motivation and encouragement. Join financial independence communities, attend workshops, and connect with others who share your goals. Surrounding yourself with supportive people can help you stay focused and motivated.

Adjusting plans as needed is important for staying on track. Life is unpredictable, and your financial situation may change over time. Regularly review your goals and adjust your plan to reflect any changes in your circumstances. Stay flexible and be prepared to make adjustments as needed.

The impact of financial freedom on life can be profound. Achieving financial independence can provide you with the freedom to pursue your passions, spend more time with loved ones, and enjoy a higher quality of life. Financial freedom can reduce stress, increase happiness, and provide a sense of security.

This chapter has provided an overview of the steps to achieve financial independence and enjoy the benefits of financial freedom. By setting goals, saving, investing, and making smart financial decisions, you can build wealth and create the life you want. Stay focused, stay disciplined, and enjoy the journey to financial freedom.

Chapter 13: Continuing Your Financial Journey

Your financial journey doesn't end once you achieve your initial goals. Continuing to manage and grow your finances is an ongoing process that requires regular attention and adjustment. This chapter will guide you through the steps to maintain and build upon your financial success, ensuring long-term stability and growth.

Recap of key concepts covered in this book highlights the importance of understanding money, budgeting, saving, investing, and protecting your finances. These foundational principles are essential for managing your money effectively and achieving your financial goals.

Ongoing financial education is crucial for staying informed and making smart decisions. The financial world is constantly changing, and new opportunities and challenges arise. Continuously educate yourself through books, articles, workshops, and courses to stay up-to-date with the latest trends and best practices.

Using technology for financial management can simplify the process and provide valuable insights. There are many tools and apps available to help you track your spending, manage your investments, and plan for the future. Find the tools that work best for you and integrate them into your financial routine.

Finding reliable financial resources is important for getting accurate information and advice. Look for reputable sources, like financial advisors, government websites, and established financial publications. Be cautious of information from unknown or unverified sources.

The role of financial advisors can be invaluable in helping you manage and grow your money. A financial advisor can provide personalized advice, help you create and adjust your financial plan, and offer insights into complex financial matters. When choosing a financial advisor, look for someone with experience, credentials, and a good track record.

Joining financial communities can provide support and motivation. Whether it's online forums, local clubs, or social media groups, connecting with others who share your financial goals can be inspiring and helpful. Share your experiences, ask questions, and learn from others in the community.

Staying motivated is key to maintaining your financial success. Set new goals, celebrate your achievements, and remind yourself of the benefits of financial stability. Surround yourself with supportive people who encourage and inspire you to stay on track.

Adapting to changes in life is an important part of continuing your financial journey. Life is unpredictable, and your financial situation may change over time. Be prepared to adjust your goals and plans as needed to reflect any changes in your circumstances.

Setting new financial goals is essential for continued growth. Once you achieve your initial goals, set new ones to keep yourself motivated and focused. Whether it's saving for a new house, starting a business, or planning for early retirement, having clear goals can help you stay on track.

Staying disciplined is crucial for maintaining your financial success. This means sticking to your budget, avoiding unnecessary spending, and making consistent contributions to your savings and investments. Discipline and consistency are essential for long-term financial stability.

The importance of review and adjustment cannot be overstated. Regularly review your financial plan, budget, and investments to ensure they still align with your goals. Make adjustments as needed to stay on track and respond to changes in your financial situation.

Celebrating financial successes can help you stay motivated and enjoy the journey. Set smaller goals along the way and celebrate when you reach them. This can make the process of managing your finances more enjoyable and rewarding.

Learning from financial mistakes is an important part of continuing your financial journey. Everyone makes mistakes, but the key is to learn from them and make better decisions in the future. Reflect on your experiences, identify areas for improvement, and make changes to avoid repeating the same mistakes.

Teaching others about personal finance can be rewarding and reinforce your own knowledge. Share your experiences and insights with friends, family, and your community. By helping others improve their financial literacy, you can contribute to a more financially secure and informed society.

Building a financial legacy involves creating a plan for the future. This might include setting up trusts, making charitable donations, or passing on family businesses or property. Proper planning can ensure your assets are used in a way that aligns with your values and provides for your loved ones.

The impact of financial stability on life is significant. Achieving financial stability can reduce stress, increase happiness, and provide a sense of security. It allows you to focus on your passions, spend more time with loved ones, and enjoy a higher quality of life.

Giving back is an important aspect of continuing your financial journey. Consider ways to use your financial success to make a positive impact on others. This might include charitable donations, volunteering, or mentoring others in their financial journey.

Staying humble with money is crucial for maintaining perspective and making wise decisions. No matter how successful you become, it's important to remember the value of money and the importance of using it responsibly. Stay grounded, be generous, and make thoughtful choices.

Planning for the future involves setting new goals and creating a plan to achieve them. Whether it's saving for a new house, starting a business, or planning for early retirement, having clear goals can help you stay focused and motivated. Regularly review and adjust your plan to ensure it aligns with your changing circumstances.

Balancing enjoyment and saving is key to a fulfilling financial journey. While it's important to save and invest for the future, it's also important to enjoy the present. Find a balance that allows you to enjoy life while still working towards your financial goals.

Financial resilience is the ability to recover from setbacks and continue moving forward. Life is unpredictable, and your financial situation may change over time. Building resilience involves creating a financial cushion, staying flexible, and being prepared to adapt to changes.

Seeking professional help when needed can provide valuable insights and support. Financial advisors, insurance agents, and other professionals can help you make informed decisions and protect your finances. Don't hesitate to reach out for help when needed.

Encouraging financial literacy in your community can have a positive impact. Share your knowledge and experiences with others, and support initiatives that promote financial education. By helping others improve their financial literacy, you can contribute to a more financially secure and informed society.

Final thoughts and encouragement remind you that managing your finances is an ongoing journey. Stay focused on your goals, stay disciplined, and continue to educate yourself. The effort you put into managing your money will pay off in the form of financial stability, security, and freedom.

By following the principles and strategies outlined in this book, you can achieve your financial goals and enjoy the benefits of financial success. Stay committed to your financial journey, and remember that the power to shape your financial future is in your hands.

www.ingramcontent.com/pod-product-compliance
Lightning Source LLC
Chambersburg PA
CBHW072018230526
45479CB00008B/290